O BVDA VÁROS
B.

1723

Pest, 1687?

1873

D0468018

BUDAPEST

BUDAPEST

Introduction by Balázs Dercsényi

MERHÁVIA · HUNGARIAN PICTURES

Pictures selected and designed by *Judit Löblin*

Published jointly by Magyar Képek Kiadói Ltd., Budapest and
Merhávia Ltd., Budapest (1139 Budapest, Teve u. 41., Hungary)

Translated by *László Jakabfi*

Photos: Magyar Képek Ltd., photo archives

Lóránt Bérczi: 138
Csaba Gábler: 7, 39, 71, 77, 78, 79, 80, 82, 99, 147, 149, 174, 192,
205, 206, 209, 219
Csaba Gedai: 148, 210, 212, 213, 222
Tibor Hortobágyi: Front Cover, Tables, 1, 4, 5, 6, 9, 11, 23, 25, 28, 29, 30,
31, 33, 34, 35, 38, 40, 44, 46, 56, 57, 58, 59, 63, 64, 66, 76, 100, 109, 110, 112,
113, 116, 118, 127, 129, 150, 155, 156, 158, 164, 165, 166, 167, 168, 169, 171,
178, 180, 184, 185, 191, 196, 197, 198, 202, 211, 214, 215, 225
Tibor Inkey: 45, 139, 173
Lajos Köteles: 87, 88
Attila Mudrák: 119
Endre Pál: 24, 27, 36, 37, 41, 42, 43, 89, 90, 91
Csaba Raffael: Back Cover, 26, 55, 60, 134
Herbert Saphier: 2, 3, 61, 65, 86, 97, 133, 163, 218
Miklós Sehr: 60, 67, 106, 140, 161, 195, 200, 201, 208
Károly Szelényi: 20, 21, 22, 32, 47, 48, 49, 50, 51, 52, 53, 62, 70, 72, 73, 74, 75,
85, 92, 93, 101, 102, 103, 104, 105, 106, 107, 108, 111, 114, 115, 117, 120, 121,
122, 123, 124, 125, 126, 128, 130, 131, 132, 135, 136, 137, 141, 142, 143, 144,
145, 146, 151, 152, 153, 154, 157, 159, 160, 170, 172, 175, 176, 177, 181, 182,
183, 187, 188, 189, 190, 193, 194, 199, 203, 204, 216, 217, 220, 221, 223, 224
László Török: 14
Ferenc Tulok: 8, 10, 12, 13, 15, 16, 17, 18, 19, 54, 69, 81, 83, 84, 94, 95, 96, 98,
162, 179, 207

Colour separation: Color Point Ltd., Budapest, 1993
Printed in Hungary by Pauker Nyomda Ltd., Budapest, 2004

ISBN 963 7587 97 7

I'd like just to waylay the owner of this beautiful book for a few short moments while I add one or two introductory thoughts, because although I'm convinced that the two hundred and fifty colour photographs which follow will more than adequately reflect the Budapest of today, a few words must be said about the historical layers which–be they hidden or spectacularly apparent–have defined the modern face of this two thousand-year-old city.

The oldest, or if you prefer the lowermost layer is that of the Roman era. Between the 13th and 9th centuries before Christ, the armies of Emperor Augustus occupied the territories to the West and South of the Danube and set up the province of Pannonia. On both the right and left banks of the river they built up the fortified boundaries protecting the Empire from Barbarian assault, one of the strategic points being the garrison town of Aquincum. The plentiful remains of the dual town which flourished in the 2nd century A.D. can be admired today in the Northern area of the Buda side of known as Óbuda, but the town performed a far more significant function at the time of the birth of the Hungarian state.

This then is the next layer of the city's history, the first of the Middle Ages. The reigning Hungarian princes, from the end of the 9th century, settled into the amphitheatre of the former Roman garrison town, whose high walls provided adequate protection. The first seeds of the town of Pest were also sown at that time, where the walls of Contra-Aquincum stood protecting the most important crossing point at the harbour of Tabán. Further increasing the significance of Óbuda, traders and craftsmen set up shop among the remains of the Roman town–or at least with the use of them–and a Royal Court, monasteries and churches were built alongside.

It was the same in Pest, although up on the Castle Hill of Buda quiet still reigned. The first golden age of Óbuda and Pest then came to an end with the invasion (in 1241) and terrible destruction and slaughter by the Tartars. The reconstruction constituted the next great period. In the interests of effective defence, the Castle Hill was occupied, with houses, churches and monastic buildings handling under the protection of the castle walls. Of course Óbuda and Pest were also rebuilt and the "triple city", now risen again from the ashes, created the suitable conditions for a royal seat to be established at the southern end of the Castle Hill some one hundred years later. For two hundred years, more and more splendid palaces were built, adorned with works of Gothic renaissance art ranking among the best in Europe.

Then for nearly a century and a half, from the dawn of modern history in 1541 until 1686, the Turks held possession of Buda and Pest. The magnificent royal palace, the town houses and monasteries gradually fell into ruin, the Christian temples being replaced by mosques and the silhouette of the town diversified by slender minarettes and domed bath-houses.

Following the victory of the united Christian armies, baroque towns appear in the first half of the 18th century, the traces of which are still discernible today. Town houses, palaces of the nobility, public buildings, parish and monastic churches were built, and the squares were graced with statues. The widest opportunities for development were enjoyed by Pest, while Buda became a quiet provincial town and Óbuda, as the seigniorial centre, a market town.

In the first half of the 19th century, an abrupt leap in development was unequivocally felt in Pest. Through a calculated programme of urban planning, neo-classical public buildings, mansions, town houses and churches sprung up. The town had far outgrown the proportions of a medieval village, and through the selfless efforts of the "greatest Hungarian" István Széchenyi, the long-awaited permanent link between the two cities came about by means of the construction of the Chain Bridge. By the middle of the century Pest was effectively the centre of the nation.

With the unification of the three towns in 1872, the city of Budapest thereby created became in the closing decades of the last century not merely a capital, but–by the scale and dimensions of that time–a metropolis. Not only was it an administrative capital for the Hungary of that time a country considerably larger then than it is now but a centre of industry, trade, communications, intellectual and artistic life, education and last but not least architecture, a fact which the boulevards and avenues, public and religious buildings, aristocratic mansions, apartment houses, banks, schools, universities and so on bear ample witness to. This metropolis, growing up in the eclectic and then Art Nouveau style, led a flourishing and radiant life, perceptible and influential throughout almost all points of the Carpathian basin, right up until the outbreak of World War I.

At that time, and even more so today, the layers of history can be felt and enjoyed: the city has an eclectic character, not merely in the architectural or historical sense, but rather in that ancient, medieval and modern values sit comfortably side by side. In a modern environment, the remnants of the province of Pannonia, along with the medieval fragments of baroque houses, and the baroque churches and neo-classical palaces nestling among eclectic and Art Nouveau buildings, all gather together under the shadow of modern hotels. All this can be relished in this magnificent book.

◁◁ **1** Coat of arms with the crown on Liberty bridge, built between 1894–1896

◁ **2** Part of the Budapest Danube embankment–registered in the UNESCO list of World Heritages–together with the Fishermen's Bastion, Viziváros (Waterside town) district and Parliament

3 The Buda Castle complex of buildings together with Chain bridge built in neoclassicist style. The Chain bridge was opened to the general public in 1849

4 The so-called 'Great Hungarian' coat of arms on the mosaic made in 1880 and positioned at the eastern entrance to the Tunnel

5 Kilometre stone 0 and the funicular railway that has run almost continuously since 1860

6 The neoclassicist-style gate to the Tunnel, opened in 1855, and leading under the Castle Hill, together with the funicular railway

7

8

7 The one-time prime minister's mansion with the northern neo-Baroque ornate fence of the Royal Palace

8 Summer mood in Tárnok utca, the burgher town district in Buda

9 The northern neo-Baroque ornate fence and gate of the Royal Palace

10 End of Tárnok utca and Szentháromság tér (Holy Trinity square)

11 Szentháromság column erected in the early 18th century, and the neo-Gothic spire of Matthias Church

12 Detail of the southern facade of Matthias Church

13 Roof covered with glazed tiles of the main church in Buda Castle district

14 A trip by hansom, the most pleasant sightseeing "service" in the Buda Castle district, sets out from Szentháromság tér

15 The main portal to Matthias Church

16 Szentháromság column and the southern facade of Matthias Church

17–21 Details of the Fishermen's Bastion and the ornamental staircase constructed from 1895 to 1902 rising above city walls in the 18th century, together with an equestrian statue of Hungary's first king, St. Stephen

22

23

24

25

26 ▷

22 The spire of the medieval church for monks of the Dominican order with a memorial portraying King Matthias

23 The multi-faceted Hilton Hotel: the medieval church spire is surrounded by 18th-century and modern wings with a statue of Pope Innocent IX

24 Old and new blend well: walls of the sanctuary of the 13th-century church built by the Dominican order and the modern wing of Hilton Hotel, part of the Budapest skyline, together with the statue of brothers Gellért and Juliánus. The brothers were commissioned with discovering the roots of the ancient Magyars

25 18th-century burgher houses and the Erdődy mansion in Táncsics utca

26 Matthias Church as seen from Tóth Árpád sétány (promenade)

27 The Buda Town Hall built in the 18th century

28 A burgher's house built in the late 18th century in Szentháromság utca with the famous Ruszwurm confectionery

29 Gothic arcades in the courtyard of the building at Országház utca 2

30 The courtyard facade of Erdődy mansion (Táncsics utca 7) built in late Baroque style

△ 27
29

28

30

31 Lions holding a shield with coat of arms in the medieval block of buildings at Úri utca 13

32 A statue of Hussar Captain András Hadik outside the Buda Town Hall in Úri utca

33 Gothic sediles under the gateway of the building in Úri utca 32

34 A Baroque burgher's house adorned with murals and magnificent latticework in Táncsics utca 16

31

33

32 △

34

35

36

37

38

39

40

35 The neoclassicist-styled Nádor barracks built in 1847, used as the Museum of War History today

36 Part of Tóth Árpád promenade

37 A sink-stone on Tóth Árpád promenade is a masterpiece from the renowned Zsolnay factory, donated by the town of Pécs and Baranya county to Budapest when it marked the centenary of its unification in 1973

38 The spire of the medieval Mary Magdalene Church, destroyed in World War II, and the restored window of its sanctuary

39 Remnants of the Mary Magdalene Church built in the 13–15th centuries in Kapisztrán tér

40 A nun praying at the corner of the late Baroque building in Petermann bíró utca 4

41 Burgher houses built at the turn of the 18–19th centuries and the neo-Roman building of the Hungarian National Archives

42 Kard utca with the Lutheran church

43 A late Baroque corner-house (Bécsi kapu tér 8), built around 1800, with medieval details

44 Baroque-style burgher houses (Országház utca 20–22) with medieval details

45 An equestrian statue dedicated to Prince Eugene of Savoy, commander in chief of the combined Christian forces that recaptured Buda Castle from Ottoman rule in 1686, outside the Royal Palace overlooking the Danube

46 The medieval courtyard in the palace and the Budapest Museum of History

47 The Royal Palace is a cultural centre nowadays housing museums and the National Széchényi Library. This picture shows the Hungarian National Gallery

48 Remnant of a statue of an elegant knight from the first third of the 15th-century on display at the Budapest Museum of History

49 One of the halls of the Hungarian National Gallery, with an exhibition of 19th-century Hungarian painting

50 *Skylark,* by Pál Szinyei Merse from 1883

51 *The Swing,* by Pál Szinyei Merse from 1869

52 *Cökxpön,* by Lajos Gulácsy

53 *Woman with Cage,* by József Rippl-Rónai from 1892

48
▽ 49

50

51

52

53

54 The central section of the Castle Garden bazaar built in 1872 on the designs of Miklós Ybl, and the southeastern wing of the Royal Palace

55 A view over the Castle Garden bazaar and on the 19th-century and modern buildings lining the Pest embankment of the Danube

56 A front view to the neo-Renaissance Castle Garden bazaar

57 Castle Garden kiosk, a building constructed from 1874–1879 on the designs of Miklós Ybl, originally served the water supply of the Palace before being turned into a pleasant restaurant. Today it is a casino

58 The ornamental main entry to the neo-Renaissance-style Castle Garden kiosk

54

▽ 55

59 The Big Round Bastion and the Gatehouse guarding the one-time medieval Royal Palace

60 The Royal Palace viewed from the south together with the medieval mace-shaped tower, the Big Round Bastion and the Gatehouse

61 View from the statue of St. Gellért: the Royal Palace to the left, followed by the town quarter called Tabán and to the right Elizabeth bridge. In the background lies the central part of the Pest embankment of the Danube

62 A neo-Baroque building at Apród utca 1–3 under the Palace is the house where the physician Ignác Semmelweis was born, today of museum for medical science. The picture shows the Empire furnishings of the Holy Spirit pharmacy founded by Károly Gömöry. It was built in 1813

59

▽ 61

60

63 A statue erected in memory of Bishop St. Gellért

64 The waterfall and ornamental staircase leading up to the statue of St. Gellért

65 View from St. Gellért hill to downtown Pest

66 View of Elizabeth bridge with the parish church of Pest dating from medieval times

67 Fireworks staged on the day of St. Stephen

63

64

68 Liberty Bridge commissioned in 1896

69 Hotel Gellért, built from 1911 to 1918 in Art Nouveau style. Public baths are linked to the hotel

70–72 Details from the inside of the baths

70

71

72

73 ◁
74
75

73 Király fürdő (Royal Baths) built around 1570 on the orders of the Buda Pasha Sokollu Mustapha, is an intact relic of Turkish bathing culture

74 The big basin built from characteristic elements of Turkish architecture in Király fürdő

75 A view from Rózsadomb (Rose Hill), with the grave erected in memory of dervish Gül Baba (Father of the Roses) from 1543 to 1548

76 Fő tér (main square) in Óbuda

77 Remnants of the military camp of Aquincum, one of the centres of the province of Pannónia, in Óbuda. Pannónia, organised around the first century A.D. defended the Roman empire from the northeast

78 Villas were built in the surroundings of Aquincum. One of them is decorated by a mosaic from the early 3rd century presenting a scene from the legend of Hercules

76

77

78

80 △
79

79 Remnants of the amphitheatre from the burger town built in the first half of the 2nd century

80 One of the restored stretches of the aquaduct leading spring waters which gush forth from the foot of nearby hills to Aquincum

81–84 A garden of ruins and the museum exhibiting some of the remains of the burger town; the forum (picture **82**) and the macellum (meat hall, picture **84**)

81

82

83

84

85

85–93 Szentendre, just a few kilometres outside the capital, is a town of museums, Greek Orthodox ecclesiastical art relics and quaint streets. One of the museums exhibits the ceramic works of Margit Kovács (pictures **85** and **92**), the church of Blagovestenska (picture **93**) built in 1752, with a memorial cross of Serbian merchants dating from 1763 in the main square. An open-air ethnographic museum (skanzen) is under construction on the outer edges of the town. One part of its presents the folk architecture of the Upper Tisza region (picture **86**) with the Reformed church transferred from Mánd (built around 1790, picture **88**) and a belfry carved in 1666, transferred from Nemesborzova (picture **87**)

86

87

88

89

90

91

92

93 ▽

94–98 Margaret Island is the top favourite "leisure centre" for residents of Budapest with the Palatinus lido (picture **97**), parks and gardens presenting rare flora (pictures **95** and **98**), Thermál Hotel also serving curative purposes (picture **96**) and the musical well (picture **94**)

94

95

96

97

99 The Chain bridge built in neoclassicist style and Parliament built from 1884–1904 in neo-Gothic style. The impressive building acts as the "workplace" for Hungary's president, prime minister and members of Parliament

100–101 The main entrance and main staircase of Parliament

102–105 Details from Parliament: the huge canvas of Mihály Munkácsy depicting the Magyar Conquest of the homeland (1893) decorating Nándorfehérvár Hall (picture **103**) and the figurative and decorative works which richly adorn the walls and columns

106 The one-time Kúria (high court) built from 1893–1896 and hosting the Ethnographical Museum today is situated near Parliament

107 A plate decorated with birds from Mezőcsát, dating from 1843

108 A wooden chest decorated with birds

109 The adorned neo-Baroque-style central hall of the museum

106

107

108

109 ▷

110 Equestrian statue of Prince Ferenc Rákóczi II outside Parliament

111 The eternal flame in memory of Lajos Batthyány, the prime minister of the first independent Hungarian government who was executed on October 6, 1849

112 A bank built in Hungarian Art Nouveau style in Hold utca and completed in 1902

113 The neoclassicist-style Chain bridge together with buildings in Roosevelt square and the spires and cupola of St. Stephen's Basilica

114

114 A bronze statue in memory of Count István Széchenyi, often called "the greatest Hungarian", and unveiled in 1880

115 The function hall of the Academy of Sciences

116 The neo-Renaissance head-quarters of the Hungarian Academy of Sciences built from 1862–1865 from donations given by István Széchenyi

115

116

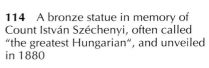

117 An Art Nouveau-style window decorated with the portrait of Lajos Kossuth in one of the staircases of the Gresham Palace

118 The office and residence of the London-based Gresham insurance company in Roosevelt square built in the Art Nouveau style from 1905–1907 on the designs of Zsigmond Quittner

117

118

119

120
▷ 121

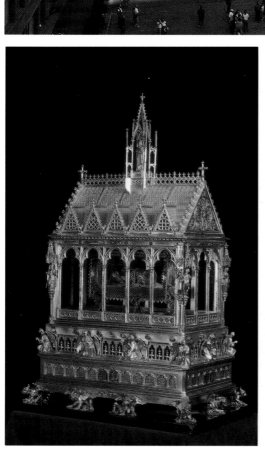

119 The parish church of King St. Stephen, the basilica in Pest, were built in neo-Renaissance style from 1851–1905 on the designs of József Hild, Miklós Ybl and József Kauser

120 The silver sacristy house, built in Vienna in 1862 on the designs of József Lippert and preserving St. Stephen's Holy Right Hand

121 Monstrance of Kolos Vaszary

122 The neo-Renaissance nave leading towards the main sanctuary

124
125

123
126

127

123–127 Parts of downtown Budapest: a neo-classicist staircase (picture 123), neo-Renaissance figures on the wall and the worked door (pictures 124–125), the Danubius Well in Erzsébet tér which was completed on the designs of Miklós Ybl together with statues by Béla Brestyánszky in 1883 (pictures 126–127)

128 Prince Ferenc Rákóczi II's messenger in the Post Museum

129 A modern block of offices was recently completed on the designs of József Finta at the corner of Erzsébet tér

128

129

130 The interior of the Lutheran church in Deák tér with the main altar designed by Mihály Polláck from 1811

131 A front view of the neoclassicist church designed by Mihály Polláck and József Hild from 1796–1856

130

131

132 Interior of the Romantic-style synagogue with a replica of the Ark of the Covenant, possibly designed by Frigyes Feszl

133 The synagogue was built on the designs of Ludwig Förster between 1854–1859

134 A front view of the Hungarian National Museum designed by Mihály Polláck and built from 1837–1848

135 The function hall with the Coronation Regalia on display

136 The Hungarian Royal Crown. Its lower part was made in Byzantium from 1074–1077, and its upper part a good 100 years later, possibly in Hungary

137 The Coronation Robe was made as a vestment in the convent of Greek nuns in the valley of Veszprém in 1031

138 A Gothic choir stall carved in 1483, originating from the St.Giles church in Bártfa (Bardejov, Slovakia), today on display at the Hungarian National Museum

136

138

137

139

140

▷ 141

139 A group of figures paying tribute to the poet János Arany by Alajos Strobl in the garden before the central part of the museum

140 A memorial dedicated to "the founders of Hungarian archeology" in the museum garden

141 The Károlyi garden with the so-called University church which took nearly 50 years to build starting from 1725, and the Károlyi mansion dating from the 1830s

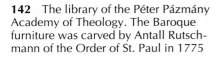

143

142 The library of the Péter Pázmány Academy of Theology. The Baroque furniture was carved by Antall Rutschmann of the Order of St. Paul in 1775

143 Ornamental gateway to a downtown block of flats dating from the last third of the 19th century

144 The Greek Orthodox church in Szerb utca, downtown Pest, from the first third of the 18th century

145 Gravestones in the wall of the Serbian church

146 An atmospheric small restaurant in Kecskeméti utca

147 Hotel Korona in Kálvin tér

148 A view from the ground floor of the Museum of Applied Arts

149 Part of the museum's roof covered with glazed tiles

150 A front view to the Museum of Applied Arts built in Art Nouveau style from 1893–1896 on the designs of Ödön Lechner and Gyula Pártos

148

149

150

151–153 The treasures of the Museum of Applied Arts: The Natuilus chalice (picture **151**), a Czech etched glass from the middle of the 19th century (picture **152**) and a tapestry portraying a mythological scene (picture **153**)

151

152

153 ▷

154

156

154 The New York cafe dating from late last century

155 The Academy of Music built in the early years of the 20th century on the designs of Kálmán Giergl and Flóris Korb together with a statue of Ferenc Liszt

156 The vestibule of the Academy of Music in Art Nouveau style

157 Glass window by Miksa Róth from the Ernst Museum

158 Art's Spring, by Aladár Körösfői-Kriesch. A fresco from the Academy of Music dating from 1907

157

158

159 Front view of the neo-Renaissance-style Opera built from 1875–1884, based on the designs of Miklós Ybl

160 Detail of a coffered fresco

161 The ceiling of the auditorium decorated with a painting by Károly Lotz

162–163 The main staircase and the auditorium

161

162

163

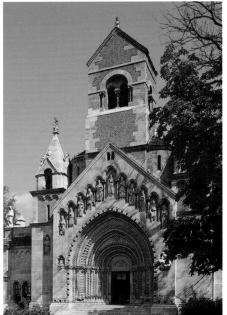

164 The so-called Vajdahunyad vár castle, a complex of prominent art relics compiled from various ages on the designs of Ignác Alpár from 1896–1902, stands on the Széchenyi island in City Park lake. The castle houses the Museum of Agriculture today

165 Bridge crossing over the City Park lake and the Millennium Memorial dedicated to the 1000th anniversary of Hungary's existence as a state

166 Gothic dome facade with the Torture tower in Vajdahunyad vár castle

167 Dome facade with Nyebojsza tower

168 A replica of the portal to the church at Ják

169 A Baroque palace with the Apostles tower

170 The Gundel restaurant

171 The neo-Baroque Széchenyi spa bath was built from 1909–1913 on the designs of Győző Czigler

172 Details from the zoo built from 1908 onwards

173 A statue dating from 1903 portraying Anonymus, an unidentified chronicler of Hungary, in City Park. It is the work of Miklós Ligeti

170

171

172

173

174

175

178

174 The Museum of Fine Arts built from 1900–1906 on the designs of Albert Schickedanz

175–177 From the treasures of the Museum of Fine Arts: *Portrait of a Youth,* by Raffaello (picture **175**), *Man's Head,* by El Greco (picture **176**), *Grinder,* by Goya (picture **177**),

178 The Millennium Memorial by György Zala, built from 1891–1898

179 The Art Gallery built on the designs of Albert Schickedanz in 1895

180 The Well of Danaides, by Ferenc Sidló

181 Atlas carrying the globe on his shoulders together with figures symbolising war and peace on the main facade of the House of Invalids (now the Budapest Mayor's Office), built from 1716 onwards

182 The early Baroque main facade of the House of Invalids and the Church of Servites

▽ 181

183

183 A mosaic adorning the facade of the Turkish Bank erected in 1906

184 △

184 Kristóf tér in the downtown

185 The county seat of Pest built from 1838–1841 on the designs of Mátyás Zitterbarth junior

185

186   The Well of Nereides on Ferenciek tere

187   A relief paying tribute to Baron Miklós Wesselényi, the hero who saved flood victims in 1838, on the wall of the Franciscan church in Pest

188   The interior of the Franciscan church erected between 1727–1743 and replacing a Turkish mosque

189   Ferenciek tere and Kossuth Lajos utca running off into the distance

190   Part of the facade of a building in Kígyó utca

191   Párizsi udvar (courtyard) leads through the ground floor of the bank built in Art Nouveau style from 1909–1913

192   The bank building constructed on the designs of Henrik Schmal in Ferenciek tere, with the Klotild mansion

190
▷ 191
192

193 A modern-looking Elizabeth bridge leading right into the heart of downtown Pest

194 The Péterffy mansion built in 1755 is a fine and rare relic of middle class Baroque architecture in downtown Pest

195 A statue of the poet Sándor Petőfi on the Danube embankment

196 The main facade of the parish church in the downtown area together with a well-house

197 Remnants of the nearly 2000-year-old fortress of Contra Aquincum together with Pest's medieval parish church

198 Váci utca as seen from Elizabeth bridge

199 Marzipan figures and ice-cream specialities are offered in this store in Párizsi utca

200–201 Hermes Well in the pedestrian street outside the Fontana store

198
▽ 200

199
201 ▽

202 Part of a facade with neo-Gothic elements

203 'Philanthia' flower shop dating from 1906, built on the designs of Albert Körössy, with an Art Nouveau interior featuring a painting by Lajos Márk

204 The Art Nouveau portal of 'Philanthia' flower shop

202

203

204

205–210 Vörösmarty tér with Gerbeaud mansion (picture **205**). The
famous Gerbeaud confectionery
(picture **206**). A statue paying tribute to
the poet Mihály Vörösmarty (picture
207). Moments in the square (pictures
208–210)

205 ◁
206
207 ▽

211 Modern architecture in the old town quarter: Corvinus-Kempinsky Hotel in the downtown

212–214 The Budapest Bank reflects elegance, authority and a respect for traditions

211
▷ 212

213
▷ 214

215 The Hungarian and Romantic-style Vigadó (Redoute) built from 1858–1865 on the designs of Frigyes Feszl

216–221 Moods on the Danube promenade: Atrium Hyatt and Forum Hotels along the Pest embankment of the Danube (picture **218**)

222 The Las Vegas casino is housed in the Atrium Hyatt Hotel

223 Sculptures symbolising music and dance on the main facade of the Vigadó

224 The Danube promenade with the Vigadó and the Basilica towering over the downtown area

220 ▷
223 ▷

215

221 ▷

216 ◁
217

222 ▷
224 ▷

218 ◁
219

Óbud

Buda, 1703

Budap